Hand in Hand

Also by Carol Ann Duffy

Standing Female Nude (1985)

Selling Manhattan (1987)

The Other Country (1990)

Mean Time (1993)

Penguin Selected Poems (1994)

The World's Wife (1999)

FOR CHILDREN

Meeting Midnight (1999)

Rumpelstiltskin and Other Grimm Tales (1999)

The Oldest Girl in the World (2000)

AS EDITOR

I Wouldn't Thank You for a Valentine (1992)

Stopping for Death (1996)

Anvil New Poets (1996)

Time's Tidings (1999)

Hand in Hand

An Anthology of Love Poems

EDITED BY

CAROL ANN DUFFY

PICADOR

First published 2001 by Picador
an imprint of Pan Macmillan Ltd
Pan Macmillan, 20 New Wharf Road, London N1 9RR
Basingstoke and Oxford
Associated companies throughout the world
www.panmacmillan.com

ISBN 0 330 48225 4

Editorial material copyright © Carol Ann Duffy 2001

The acknowledgements on pages 105–10 constitute an extension of
this copyright page.

5 7 9 8 6 4

A CIP catalogue record for this book is available from
the British Library.

Typeset by SetSystems Ltd, Saffron Walden, Essex
Printed and bound in Great Britain by
Mackays of Chatham plc, Chatham, Kent

Contents

vii

Foreword

How do I love thee? Let me count the ways ... So wrote
Elizabeth Barrett Browning to Robert Browning in one of the
best-known, and best-loved, of English love poems. When we
fall in love it's often to our poets that we turn, sending a book
of poetry to the beloved, like the adulterous husband with his
first edition of e. e. cummings in Woody Allen's *Hannah and
Her Sisters* or carefully copying out a particular poem by hand
... *I love thee to the depth and breadth and height / My soul
can reach* ... and posting it off to the *raison d'être*. For some
poets, falling in love themselves and writing their first love poem
is the start of their poetic vocation. For others, the love poem is
the brightest star in the constellation of their work. Even in
schools, on St Valentine's Day, whole classrooms sit down and
try their inky hands at a love poem. And popular song, in the
best of its lyrics, provides a singable love poetry known by heart
by millions.

In this anthology of love poems, published for St Valentine's
Day, I have invited an equal number of male and female poets
to contribute a love poem of their own which appears alongside
their favourite love poem written by a poet of the opposite sex.
I was interested in gathering together a broad range of lovers'
voices and experiences, of differing sexualities and histories in a
celebration and an exploration of love. I was curious to see what
spoke to women writers in love poetry by men and vice versa.
Some of the poems are broken-hearted and some are weak-
kneed, some are exhilarated and some are exhausted, some are
lofty and some are lusty. They have been written at very different
times – from the beginning of the sixteenth century to the start
of the twenty-first – and by very different poets. Reading the

results, I was struck not only by how many ways there are to write a love poem – *with the breath, / Smiles, tears, of all my life* – but also how many ways there are of experiencing love. Hugh MacDiarmid's 'Back Bedroom', unkempt and grey, harbours a miraculous love-making; Rosemary Tonks' 'Story of a Hotel Room' a ruinous one. Muriel Stuart's 'In the Orchard', with its sadly cross-purposed lovers, could perhaps have done with Chase Twichell's 'The Condom Tree' growing there. Selima Hill's 'Coition' (*'like a nude with a rat'*) sounds an altogether more dangerous affair than Nuala Ní Dhomhnaill's lyrical lesbian 'Labysheedy (The Silken Bed)'.

I was fascinated, as the poems arrived with the frequency of the correspondence in an affair, with the choices made by the poets. Christopher Logue, once he had rigorously clarified what exactly I meant by a love poem, selected Anne Ridler's fine and true 'A Letter':

> It is the hardest thing with love to burn
> And write it down, for what was the real passion
> Left to its own words will seem trivial and thin.
> We can in making love look face to face:
> In poetry, crooked, and with no embrace.

Kathleen Jamie protested that writing love poetry gave her 'the dry bolk' but was persuaded to allow her own lovely 'Perfect Day' to accompany her choice of Michael Longley's 'The Linen Industry'. Both poems share a tender reticence. Jackie Kay, Liz Lochhead and Carol Rumens all selected a poem by Robert Burns. Elizabeth Barrett Browning, to my surprise, was not chosen by any of the men although her husband was selected by U. A. Fanthorpe. Most poets chose poems by writers from earlier times although a few, as with Hugo Williams' choice of Eva Salzman, selected a contemporary.

I hope that readers will enjoy the poems by the living poets here and take pleasure from their choices. It is always tempting when reading such an anthology to note those poems which are missing – there are none of Shakespeare's sonnets here, for example – and it would be possible, using the same procedure, to produce a completely different selection. What follows is one intriguing route through the experience of love in all its grief and glory. Happy Valentine's Day.

CAROL ANN DUFFY

FLEUR ADCOCK

An Illustration to Dante

Here are Paolo and Francesca
whirled around in the circle of Hell
clipped serenely together
her dead face raised against his.
I can feel the pressure of his arms
like yours about me, locking.

They float in a sea of whitish blobs –
fire, is it? It could have been
hail, said Ruskin, but Rossetti
'didn't know how to do hail'.
Well, he could do tenderness.
My spine trickles with little white flames.

JOHN DONNE

Song

Sweetest love, I do not goe,
   For wearinesse of thee,
Nor in hope the world can show
   A fitter Love for mee;
     But since that I
Must dye at last, 'tis best,
To use my selfe in jest
   Thus by fain'd deaths to dye;

Yesternight the Sunne went hence,
   And yet is here to day,
He hath no desire nor sense,
   Nor halfe so short a way:
     Then feare not mee,
But beleeve that I shall make
Speedier journeyes, since I take
   More wings and spurres then hee.

O how feeble is mans power,
   That if good fortune fall,
Cannot adde another houre,
   Nor a lost houre recall!
     But come bad chance,
And wee joyne to'it our strength,
And wee teach it art and length,
   It selfe o'r us to'advance.

When thou sigh'st, thou sigh'st not winde,
   But sigh'st my soule away,
When thou weep'st, unkindly kinde,
   My lifes blood doth decay.
     It cannot bee
That thou lov'st mee, as thou say'st,
If in thine my life thou waste,
   Thou art the best of mee.

Let not thy divining heart
   Forethinke me any ill,
Destiny may take thy part,
   And may thy feares fulfill;
     But thinke that wee
Are but turn'd aside to sleepe;
They who one another keepe
   Alive, ne'r parted bee.

Chosen by Fleur Adcock

A Bowl of Warm Air

Someone is falling towards you
as an apple falls from a branch,
moving slowly, imperceptibly as if
into a new political epoch,
or excitedly like a dog towards a bone.
He is holding in both hands
everything he knows he has –
a bowl of warm air.

He has sighted you from afar
as if you were a dramatic crooked tree
on the horizon and he has seen you close up
like the underside of a mushroom.
But he cannot open you like a newspaper
or put you down like a newspaper.

And you are satisfied that he is veering towards you
and that he is adjusting his speed
and that the sun and the wind and rain are in front of him
and the sun and the wind and rain are behind him.

Come Back

Come back often and take hold of me,
sensation that I love, come back and take hold of me –
when the body's memory revives
and an old longing passes through the blood,
when lips and skin remember
and hands feel as though they touch again.

Come back often, take hold of me in the night
when lips and skin remember . . .

Chosen by Moniza Alvi

To His Lost Lover

Now they are no longer
any trouble to each other

he can turn things over, get down to that list
of things that never happened, all of the lost

unfinishable business,
For instance . . . for instance,

how he never clipped and kept her hair, or drew a hairbrush
through that style of hers, and never knew how not to blush

at the fall of her name in close company.
How they never slept like buried cutlery –

two spoons or forks cupped perfectly together,
or made the most of some heavy weather –

walking out into hard rain under sheet lightning,
or did the gears while the other was driving.

How he never raised his fingertips
to stop the segments of her lips

from breaking the news,
or tasted the fruit,

or picked for himself the pear of her heart,
or lifted her hand to where his own heart

was a small, dark, terrified bird
in her grip. Where it hurt.

Or said the right thing,
or put it in writing.

And never fled the black mile back to his house
before midnight, or coaxed another button of her blouse,

then another,
or knew her

favourite colour,
her taste, her flavour,

and never ran a bath or held a towel for her,
or soft-soaped her, or whipped her hair

into an ice-cream cornet or a beehive
of lather, or acted out of turn, or misbehaved

when he might have, or worked a comb
where no comb had been, or walked back home

through a black mile hugging a punctured heart,
where it hurt, where it hurt, or helped her hand

to his butterfly heart
in its two blue halves.

And never almost cried,
and never once described

an attack of the heart,
or under a silk shirt

nursed in his hand her breast,
her left, like a tear of flesh

wept by the heart,
where it hurts,

or brushed with his thumb the nut of her nipple,
or drank intoxicating liquors from her navel.

Or christened the Pole Star in her name,
or shielded the mask of her face like a flame,

a pilot light,
or stayed the night,

or steered her back to that house of his,
or said 'Don't ask me to say how it is

I like you.
I just might do.'

How he never figured out a fireproof plan,
or unravelled her hand, as if her hand

were a solid ball
of silver foil

and discovered a lifeline hiding inside it,
and measured the trace of his own alongside it.

But said some things and never meant them –
sweet nothings anybody could have mentioned.

And left unsaid some things he should have spoken,
about the heart, where it hurt exactly, and how often.

STEVIE SMITH

Infelice

Walking swiftly with a dreadful duchess,
He smiled too briefly, his face was as pale as sand,
He jumped into a taxi when he saw me coming,
Leaving me alone with a private meaning,
He loves me so much, my heart is singing.
Later at the Club when I rang him in the evening
They said: Sir Rat is dining, is dining, is dining,
No Madam, he left no message, ah how his silence speaks,
He loves me too much for words, my heart is singing.
The Pullman seats are here, the tickets for Paris, I am waiting,
Presently the telephone rings, it is his valet speaking,
Sir Rat is called away, to Scotland, his constituents,
(Ah the dreadful duchess, but he loves me best)
Best pleasure to the last, my heart is singing.
One night he came, it was four in the morning,
Walking slowly upstairs, he stands beside my bed,
Dear darling, lie beside me, it is too cold to stand speaking,
He lies down beside me, his face is like the sand,
He is in a sleep of love, my heart is singing.
Sleeping softly softly, in the morning I must wake him,
And waking he murmurs, I only came to sleep.
The words are so sweetly cruel, how deeply he loves me,
I say them to myself alone, my heart is singing.
Now the sunshine strengthens, it is ten in the morning,
He is so timid in love, he only needs to know,
He is my little child, how can he come if I do not call him,
I will write and tell him everything, I take the pen and write:
I love you so much, my heart is singing.

Chosen by Simon Armitage

SEAN O'BRIEN

Indian Summer

These iron comforts, reasonable taboos
(John Ashbery)

Look at this frosty red rose leaning over
The milk on the step. Please take it. But leave me
Its fragrance, its ice in the mind, to remember you by.
The girlfriends of afternoon drinkers
(*O the criminal classes, their bottle-tanned lasses*)
Have locked up their halters and shorts
Being practical girls, they have understood soon
What I struggle with late, getting grit in my eyes –
That the piss-palace garden is windy and dim
When the heat goes at four. It is over again.
Now the engineer turns up to service the heating
And says: *I see your bell's still bust*
From the Charon-cold depths of his anorak hood.
The dark house is a coffin of laws: early closing
But if the clocks must forever go back
To the meantime of Pluto, leave me your voice,
Its rumour at the confluence of Portugal and Spain,
From whose entwining waters rises, like a shell
Within the echo in the ear, your own supreme Creole.
If I am doomed to winter on the Campo Mediocrita
Whose high plateau becomes the windy shore
Of an ocean with only one side, to wait
Where the howling sunshine does not warm me,
Let me speak your tongue, at least –
For yours is the music the panther laments in,
Retreating to Barradon, yours is the silvery

Script of the spider at midnight,
Your diary is scandal's pleasure-ground
From which a bare instant of cleavage or leg
Is all I shall have to sustain me. And yours
Are the text and the age I should like to be acting:
You lie on the bed of the lawn, painted gold,
With the base of your spine left naked to breathe,
And now I might seal the extravagant promise
To kiss you to life with your name, if for once
You could look at me – do it now – straight
In the eye, without smiling or shaking your head.

ZSUZSA RAKOVSZKY

They Were Burning Dead Leaves

They were burning dead leaves. Must oozed with scent,
    tar bubbled and blew.
The moonlight glow behind the thistle bent
    like a torn rainbow.

The street was a forest, night slid into the heart
    of deepest autumn.
A guilty music blew the house apart
    with its fife and drum.

To have this again, just this, just the once more:
    I would sink below
autumnal earth and place my right hand in your
    hand like a shadow.

Chosen by Sean O'Brien

Song for a Stone

(after Iain Crichton Smith)

You are at the bottom of my mind
like a stone dropped once by chance in a pool
to the black belied
by a surface ruled
by a total reflection of sky.

I do not have the know of your want or why,
I do not have the know of your way.
I have only the flow
of the come what may
in the light to the front of my liquid eye.

But you have put a sadness in the blue-
green waters of my mind
for as long as we both may live.

For your time is not of the colour of mine
and the name that is on you cannot be written
over these lips in love.

IAN CRICHTON SMITH

You Are at the Bottom of My Mind

(from the Gaelic)

Without my knowing it you are at the bottom of my mind
like a visitor to the bottom of the sea
with his helmet and his two large eyes,
and I do not rightly know your appearance or your manner
after five years of showers
of time pouring between me and you:

nameless mountains of water pouring
between me hauling you on board
and your appearance and manner in my weak hands.
You went astray
among the mysterious plants of the sea-bed
in the green half-light without love,

and you will never rise to the surface
though my hands are hauling ceaselessly,
and I do not know your way at all,
you in the half-light of your sleep
haunting the bed of the sea without ceasing
and I hauling and hauling on the surface.

Chosen by Colette Bryce

KATE CLANCHY

Patagonia

I said *perhaps Patagonia*, and pictured
a peninsula, wide enough
for a couple of ladderback chairs
to wobble on at high tide. I thought

of us in breathless cold, facing
a horizon round as a coin, looped
in a cat's cradle strung by gulls
from sea to sun. I planned to wait

till the waves had bored themselves
to sleep, till the last clinging barnacles,
growing worried in the hush, had
paddled off in tiny coracles, till

those restless birds, your actor's hands,
had dropped slack into your lap,
until you'd turned, at last, to me.
When I spoke of Patagonia, I meant

skies all empty aching blue. I meant
years. I meant all of them with you.

THOMAS WYATT

They Flee from Me

They flee from me, that sometime did me seek
With naked foot, stalking in my chamber.
I have seen them gentle tame and meek,
That now are wild, and do not once remember
That sometime they put themselves in danger
To take bread at my hand, and now they range
Busily seeking in continual change

Thanked be fortune, it hath been otherwise
Twenty times better; but once in especial
In thin array, after a pleasant guise
When her loose gown did from her shoulders fall
And she me caught in her arms long and small
And therewithal, so sweetly did me kiss
And softly said: dear heart, how like you this?

It was no dream, for I lay broad waking
But all is turned now through my gentleness
Into a bitter fashion of forsaking
And I have leave to go of her goodness
And she also to use new fangledness
But since that I unkindly so am served
But would fain know what she hath deserved.

Chosen by Kate Clanchy

GILLIAN CLARKE

Gravity

After all these years
we still argue whose fault it was –
an old sweet war we return to
the times when it ought to be perfect.
Like tonight

when the owl cried in the garden
and we thought of her heartface,
her bloody claws.
The moon looked in through wet glass
and dissolved in tears

You say it was all down to poetry,
musk shampoo, the black *Biba* catsuit
buttoned to knuckles, to throat.
You say I leaned my head on your shoulder
in your dead grandmother's garden.

I say you planned it,
fetching the elm chairs from her empty house
in my first Renault 4.
We loaded them up
and went back for a last look.

So why did you draw the bolts on the back door
and lead me into the night garden?
To check the sky for Orion,
the autumn breath of the brewery,
bonfires and *Brains Dark*?

Looking up made us dizzy.
We leaned against gravity.
The planet turned a fraction
and we were done for,
falling, falling.

Solomon and the Witch

And thus declared that Arab lady:
'Last night, where under the wild moon
On grassy mattress I had laid me,
Within my arms great Solomon,
I suddenly cried out in a strange tongue
Not his, not mine.'
           Who understood
Whatever has been said, sighed, sung,
Howled, miau-d, barked, brayed, belled, yelled, cried, crowed,
Thereon replied: 'A cockerel
Crew from a blossoming apple bough
Three hundred years before the Fall,
And never crew again till now,
And would not now but that he thought,
Chance being at one with Choice at last,
All that the brigand apple brought
And this foul world were dead at last.
He that crowed out eternity
Thought to have crowed it in again.
For though love has a spider's eye
To find out some appropriate pain –
Aye, though all passion's in the glance –
For every nerve that tests a lover
With cruelties of Choice and Chance;
And when at last that murder's over
Maybe the bride-bed brings despair,
For each an imagined image brings
And finds a real image there;
Yet the world ends when these two things,

Though several, are a single light,
When oil and wick are burned in one;
Therefore a blessed moon last night
Gave Sheba to her Solomon.'

'Yet the world stays.'
                         'If that be so,
Your cockerel found us in the wrong
Although he thought it worth a crow.
Maybe an image is too strong
Or maybe is not strong enough.'
'The night has fallen; not a sound
In the forbidden sacred grove
Unless a petal hit the ground,
Nor any human sight within it
But the crushed grass where we have lain;
And the moon is wilder every minute.
O! Solomon! let us try again.'

Chosen by Gillian Clarke

Japan

Today I pass the time reading
a favorite haiku,
saying the few words over and over.

It feels like eating
the same small, perfect grape
again and again.

I walk through the house reciting it
and leave its letters falling
through the air of every room.

I stand by the big silence of the piano and say it.
I say it in front of a painting of the sea.
I tap out its rhythm on an empty shelf.

I listen to myself saying it,
then I say it without listening,
then I hear it without saying it.

And when the dog looks up at me,
I kneel down on the floor
and whisper it into each of his long white ears.

It's the one about the one-ton
temple bell
with the moth sleeping on its surface,

and every time I say it, I feel the excruciating
pressure of the moth
on the surface of the iron bell.

When I say it at the window,
the bell is the world
and I am the moth resting there.

When I say it into the mirror,
I am the heavy bell
and the moth is life with its papery wings.

And later, when I say it to you in the dark,
you are the bell,
and I am the tongue of the bell, ringing you,

and the moth has flown
from its line
and moves like a hinge in the air above our bed.

DORIANNE LAUX

Kissing

They are kissing, on a park bench,
on the edge of an old bed, in a doorway
or on the floor of a church. Kissing
as the streets fill with balloons
or soldiers, locusts or confetti, water
or fire or dust. Kissing down through
the centuries under sun or stars, a dead tree,
an umbrella, amid derelicts. Kissing
as Christ carries his cross, as Gandhi
sings his speeches, as a bullet
careens through the air toward a child's
good heart. They are kissing,
long, deep, spacious kisses, exploring
the silence of the tongue, the mute
rungs of the upper palate, hungry
for the living flesh. They are still
kissing when the cars crash and the bombs
drop, when the babies are born crying
into the white air, when Mozart bends
to his bowl of soup and Stalin
bends to his garden. They are kissing
to begin the world again. Nothing
can stop them. They kiss until their lips
swell, their thick tongues quickening
to the budded touch, licking up
the sweet juices. I want to believe
they are kissing to save the world,
but they're not. All they know
is this press and need, these two-legged

beasts, their faces like roses crushed
together and opening, they are covering
their teeth, they are doing what they have to do
to survive the worst, they are sealing
the hard words in, they are dying
for our sins. In a broken world they are
practising this simple and singular act
to perfection. They are holding
onto each other. They are kissing.

Chosen by Billy Collins

ROBERT CRAWFORD

Conjugation

I love the bigamy of it, the fling
Of marriage on top of marriage.
Marry me, Alice, marry my secrets,
Sight unseen, and marry Glasgow and Rose
Macaulay and the snell east wind.
I'll marry you and Iona and has-been,
Shall-be firths of slipways and dwammy kyles.
I do, you did, we'll do, hitched to every last
Drop of our wedding-day showers,
Downpours, reflecting us over and over,
So we'll fall in compact mirrors, blebs
As the heavens open, bride's veil, grey suit, ringing
Wet with carillons of rain.
That day seems like only tomorrow,
Present, future, pluperfect, perfect smirr
Champagning us doon the watter, on,
Launching us, conjugating each haugh,
Oxter, pinkie and lapless lug
As it will be in the beginning.

JUDITH WRIGHT

The Twins

Not because of their beauty – though they are slender
as saplings of white cedar, and long as lilies –
not because of their delicate dancing step,
or their brown hair sideways blown like the manes of fillies –
it is not for their beauty that the crowd in the street
wavers like dry leaves around them on the wind.
It is the chord, the intricate unison
of one and one, strikes home to the watcher's mind.

How sweet is the double gesture, the mirror-answer;
same hand woven in same, like arm in arm.
Salt blood like tears freshens the crowd's dry veins,
and moving in its web of time and harm
the unloved heart asks, 'Where is my reply,
my kin, my answer? I am driven and alone.'
Their serene eyes seek nothing. They walk by.
They move into the future and are gone.

Chosen by Robert Crawford

Torch Song

She stuffed it in her briefcase not to scare the crowds
and carried it for miles,
on trains, through car parks, down the rush hour streets.
It glowed a little, scorched her papers,
melted down her sandwiches, and made the world
inedible, illegible, a dangerous place.

Outside his door at last she hesitated, knew
she mustn't start a blaze
in there, was terrified of what one wisp
of smoke could signal to the air.
She left it on the pavement, went inside, and watched
as people gathered on the street all afternoon,

to warm their hands on it, to stare: a burning torch
inside a briefcase, smoking,
flaming now despite the steady rain
that specked the window so he noticed
hardly anything until the crowd began
to sing – a little out of key at first, unsteady

in the rhythm, then a harmony, a chorus,
building clear and almost
beautiful, that had him on his feet
and running, nearly through the door
before she reached him, pulled him back, pushed past, and all
without a thought that for a second she had held him.

In a heat haze, eyes that stung until they soaked
her face, she grabbed the briefcase,
burnt her fingers, clung on tight, and ran,
down back streets, alleys, over walls.
It lit her route the whole way home, kept men at bay,
until she reached her door and sat awake all night,

watched her torch as it burned brightly in the yard,
as he lay miles away,
unsettled, half remembering strangers singing,
dreamt a spark ignited curtains,
flared across his room and burst into a wall
of flame, to burn him down, to burn his whole world down.

PABLO NERUDA

We Have Lost Even

We have lost even this twilight.
No one saw us this evening hand in hand
while the blue night dropped on the world.

I have seen from my window
the fiesta of sunset in the distant mountain tops.

Sometimes a piece of sun
burned like a coin between my hands.

I remembered you with my soul clenched
in that sadness of mine that you know.

Where were you then?
Who else was there?
Saying what?
Why will the whole of love come on me suddenly
when I am sad and feel you are far away?

The book fell that is always turned to at twilight
and my cape rolled like a hurt dog at my feet.

Always, always you recede through the evenings
towards where the twilight goes erasing statues.

Chosen by Amanda Dalton

No, Go On

For years, he's gone over her parting words,
the ones she couldn't pack. They are printed

in the circles under his eyes. They come to mind
each night at 5 a.m., when the first trains start

and the moon bottles itself outside his door.
He is caught like a wheel on her shimmering track.

Over breakfast the rush hour begins and he wants
me to wait, starting another sentence that he just

lets fall away. And I'm saying: *no, go on, finish what
you were about to . . . I'm with you. I'm following so far.*

DELMORE SCHWARTZ

What Is to Be Given

What is to be given,
Is spirit, yet animal,
Colored, like heaven,
Blue, yellow, beautiful.

The blood is checkered by
So many stains and wishes,
Between it and the sky
You could not choose, for riches.

Yet let me now be careful
Not to give too much
To one so shy and fearful
For like a gun is touch.

Chosen by Maura Dooley

Static

When you pulled the t-shirt
over your stooped head
I heard the crackle of static
and imagined the soft,
invisible fur
of charged atmosphere
over the TV's
translucent imagery.

Lights out, my blind
and all-believing hands
discover the ghost
of a smile
on your invisible face;
here you are
in your skin,
shocking against mine.

The Shampoo

The still explosions on the rocks,
the lichens, grow
by spreading, gray, concentric shocks.
They have arranged
to meet the rings around the moon, although
within our memories they have not changed.

And since the heavens will attend
as long on us,
you've been, dear friend,
precipitate and pragmatical;
and look what happens. For Time is
nothing if not amenable.

The shooting stars in your black hair
in bright formation
are flocking where,
so straight, so soon?
– Come, let me wash it in this big tin basin,
battered and shiny like the moon.

Chosen by Nick Drake

Close

Lock the door. In the dark journey of our night,
two childhoods stand in the corner of the bedroom
watching the way we take each other to bits
to stare at our heart. I hear a story
told in sleep in a lost accent. You know the words.

Undress. A suitcase crammed with secrets
bursts in the wardrobe at the foot of the bed.
Dress again. Undress. You have me like a drawing,
erased, coloured in, untitled, signed by your tongue.
The name of a country written in red on my palm,

unreadable. I tell myself where I live now,
but you move in close till I shake, homeless,
further than that. A coin falls from the bedside table,
spinning its head and tails. How the hell
can I win. How can I lose. Tell me again.

Love won't give in. It makes a hired room tremble
with the pity of bells, a cigarette smoke itself
next to a full glass of wine, time ache
into space, space, wants no more talk. Now
it has me where I want me, now you, you do.

Put out the light. Years stand outside on the street
looking up to an open window, black as our mouth
which utters its tuneless vowels. The ghosts of ourselves,
behind and before us, throng in a mirror, blind,
laughing and weeping. They know who we are.

LUÍS VAZ de CAMÕES

My Errors My Loves My Unlucky Star

My errors my loves my unlucky star
these three things have been my curse.
My luck and my errors were bad enough
but love was the worst.

I have survived. But the pain
has bitten so deep in the bone
the rage and grief will not let go –
too hurt to want contentment now.

The blunders scattered through my life
are like a broken rosary.
I gave myself to fortune; fortune broke me.

Of love there is hardly a ghost left.
O who what angel of power can assuage
my terrible demon of revenge!

Translated by David Wevill

Chosen by Carol Ann Duffy

IAN DUHIG

From the Irish

According to Dinneen, a Gael unsurpassed
in lexicographical enterprise, the Irish
for moon means the white circle in a slice
of half-boiled potato or turnip. A star
is the mark on the forehead of a beast
and the sun is the bottom of a lake, or well.

Well, if I say to you your face
is like a slice of half-boiled turnip,
your hair is the colour of a lake's bottom
and at the centre of each of your eyes
is the mark of the beast, it is because
I want to love you properly, according to Dinneen.

Labysheedy (The Silken Bed)

I'd make a bed for you
in Labysheedy
in the tall grass
under the wrestling trees
where your skin
would be silk upon silk
in the darkness
when the moths are coming down.

Skin which glistens
shining over your limbs
like milk being poured
from jugs at dinnertime;
your hair is a herd of goats
moving over rolling hills,
hills that have high cliffs
and two ravines.

And your damp lips
would be as sweet as sugar
at evening and we walking
by the riverside
with honeyed breezes
blowing over the Shannon
and the fuchsias bowing down to you
one by one.

The fuchsias bending low
their solemn heads in obeisance to the beauty
in front of them
I would pick a pair of flowers
as pendant earrings
to adorn you
like a bride in shining clothes.

O I'd make a bed for you
in Labysheedy,
in the twilight hour
with evening falling slow
and what a pleasure it would be
to have our limbs entwine
wrestling
while the moths are coming down.

Chosen by Ian Duhig

The Difficulty That Is Marriage

We disagree to disagree, we divide, we differ;
Yet each night as I lie in bed beside you
And you are faraway curled up in sleep
I array the moonlit ceiling with a mosaic of question-marks;
How was it I was so lucky to have ever met you?
I am no brave pagan proud of my mortality,
Yet gladly on this changeling earth I should live for ever
If it were with you, my sleeping friend.
I have my troubles and I shall always have them
But I should rather live with you for ever
Than exchange my troubles for a changeless kingdom.
But I do not put you on a pedestal or throne;
You must have your faults but I do not see them.
If it were with you, I should live for ever.

Tell Me about It

When they mourn you over there
the way you'd want, the way you mourn
your friends;

when they're celebrating
having loved you
in Derry, Rathmullen, wherever –

birettas, candles, Latin,
all the weavings you don't believe in
but love anyway and I'll never share

for who the hell converts to
ex-Catholic? – no one will know
someone's missing you here

for ever. Whose arms,
printed with that absolute
man's stillness

when your breath calms
into my shoulder and you fall asleep
inside me, open and close

in a foreign night round nothing.
Who misses the way
you pour loose change on the bar

in a puddle of fairytale silver
and move through the night,
through everything, curious,

mischievous as a mongoose,
and never an unkind word.
I might dream

of coming over, touching
just one friend's sleeve
to whisper

'Talk about him. A bit.
The way he was, here' –
but never do it. Instead

I'll say *Yes* in my sleep
to you. To no one. You'll put
your tongue in my mouth, deep,

the way you do,
and my eyes will open
on a dark garden. I'll wake up

touching myself for you.
The alarm will stare
venomous digits. I'll hang on

to the fragile haze
of a wine-bar
when you leant over the foreign formica,

haltering my hand within your two
like the filling in a sandwich,
sashaying the skin of each finger

down to the soft web between,
over and over, a rosary of rub
and slide, as if you could solder

me to your lifeline. As if
you could take me with you.
And I'll wish you had.

Chosen by Paul Durcan

U. A. FANTHORPE

The Absent-Minded Lover's Apology

I would like you to think I love you warmly
Like brown cat yawning among sheets in the linen-cupboard.

I would like you to think I love you resourcefully
Like rooftop starlings posting chuckles down the flue.

I would like you to think I love you extravagantly
Like black cat embracing the floor when you pick up the tin-opener.

I would like you to think I love you accurately
Like Baskerville kern that fits its place to a T.

I would like you to think I love you with hurrahs and hallelujahs
Like dog whippetting at you down the intricate hillside.

I would like you to think I love you wittily
Like pottery Cox that lurks in the fruit-bowl under the Granny
    Smiths.

I would like you to think I love you pacifically and for ever
Like collared doves on the whitebeam's domestic branch.

I would like you to think I love you chronically
Like second hand solemnly circumnavigating the clock.

And O I want to love you, not in the absent tense, but in the here
    and the now
Like a present-minded lover.

ROBERT BROWNING

from One Word More

God be thanked, the meanest of his creatures
Boasts two soul-sides, one to face the world with,
One to show a woman when he loves her!

This I say of me, but think of you, Love!
This to you – yourself my moon of poets!
Ah, but that's the world's side, there's the wonder,
Thus they see you, praise you, think they know you!
There, in turn I stand with them and praise you –
Out of my own self, I dare to phrase it.
But the best is when I glide from out them,
Cross a step or two of dubious twilight,
Come out on the other side, the novel
Silent silver lights and darks undreamed of,
Where I hush and bless myself with silence.

Chosen by U. A. Fanthorpe

DAVID HART

A Dance in Two Seasons

I saw you first on that long, frail summer evening,
eating little at the picnic but sliding away
to hop and swirl and circumvent quietly alone.
(Some bold, private writing was done then,
for hope's sake.)
                        Nor have you ever spoken to me
except to whisper, 'Name the grasses'.
I have seen the deep cut graves on the cliff top.
The whole cliff is an open-mouthed skull,
the whole world is skull and the whole world's heart
is in its stony mouth.
                        Between trees giving way
so empathetically as hardly to be seen at all
you laugh as if you know something.

I see you now in what appears to be winter,
seed-pods lie broken open and crusty on the ground,
you walk hardly protected against the wind.
(Slower, shrivelled, impossible writing must be done now
for beauty's sake.)
                        The grasses are browning inside me –
Quaking Grass, Woodrush, Red Fescue, the Common Reed,
Glaucous Sedge, Marram, Bulrush, Wild Oat –
these have become my own names, waving against each other
for recognition.
                        I have noticed the sky
taking its cut of us, the whole sky promoting itself
as if finite around us,

so as to grasp and squeeze us.
                              Between trees holding their ground
in the evening of a billion years you abide
and laugh as if you know nothing. O blessed homeless light!

My Heart Burns for Him

Raja, my heart is mad for you,
I've gone mad for you,
but you have left the warm bed in my house.
Where will you find such warmth outside?
You have left me all alone,
you would eat roots and fruit outside,
come, my madman, let us go together to the forest.

Green is the green hill,
yellow are the bamboos,
green is the kalindar creeper,
karanda flowers are in my hair.
Where in the forest will I find my Raja?
My heart burns for him,
where in the forest will I find my madman?

Chosen by David Hart

A song poem of a Gond woman. The Gond people live in Central India, their song poems were recorded in the 1930s, translated and published by S. Hivale and V. Elwin (Allen & Unwin, London, 1935). I found this poem in the *Penguin Book of Oral Poetry*, edited by Ruth Finnegan, 1982. I have altered the punctuation a little, I have put in stops, commas and lower case first letters of lines. – David Hart

Coition

You'll have to lie perfectly still
like a nude with a rat;

and when I have finished,
you'll have not a hair on your head,

and everyone else in the world
will have gone to sleep.

Myself

It is more than
the deep roots of every emotion,
big or small, of every kind,
that squirm and kick like little children
somewhere inside

and more than
the deep-sea fish
of six senses and seven sins,
that waves its tail
like a night-time shadow on a window pane

more, too, than
star-dust littering the yards
of Original Sin and Karma,
passing through the obscure darkness of the potter's kiln

and more than
the oasis spring gushing from the desert sand,
melting again into foam and flowing
after filtering through strata of origins and time
with their rustle of dry grass,
and the crack in the glacier, or even exploding particles

more, too, than
the world, itself smaller
than a millet seed
in the cosmic vastnesses

and more than
the ether – fullness of the boundless void
reaching beyond billions of light years
of starlight

more, too, than
the substantiality such fullness gives,
and more than its opposing nihility,
more, too, than unknown death

more, greater,
a soundless cosmic shout!
An immensity embracing Eternity!

Myself.

Chosen by Selima Hill

KATHLEEN JAMIE

Perfect Day

I am just a woman of the shore
wearing your coat against the snow
that falls on the oyster-catchers' tracks
and on our own; falls
on the still grey waters
of Loch Morar, and on our shoulders
gentle as restraint: a perfect weight
of snow as tree-boughs
and fences bear against a loaded sky:
one flake more, they'd break.

MICHAEL LONGLEY

The Linen Industry

Pulling up flax after the blue flowers have fallen
And laying our handfuls in the peaty water
To rot those grasses to the bone, or building stooks
That recall the skirts of an invisible dancer,

We become a part of the linen industry
And follow its processes to the grubby town
Where fields are compacted into window-boxes
And there is little room among the big machines.

But even in our attic under the skylight
We make love on a bleach green, the whole meadow
Draped with material turning white in the sun
As though snow reluctant to melt were our attire.

What's passion but a battering of stubborn stalks,
Then a gentle combing out of fibres like hair
And a weaving of these into christening robes,
Into garments for a marriage or funeral?

Since it's like a bereavement once the labour's done
To find ourselves last workers in a dying trade,
Let flax be our matchmaker, our undertaker,
The provider of sheets for whatever the bed –

And be shy of your breasts in the presence of death,
Say that you look more beautiful in linen
Wearing white petticoats, the bow on your bodice
A butterfly attending the embroidered flowers.

Chosen by Kathleen Jamie

The Breakfast

That day, I filled the house with fruit,
with strawberries that shame the root –
their red hearts filled to bursting – and
with grapes, each one a swollen gland;
with melons pumped to ripeness, with
the peaches that are grown in myth
(plump and downy, blusher tints),
with mango, guava, quumquat, quince:

with food for love to breakfast on,
the juice-filled flesh, the skins that shone
like health; the tones of still-lifes by
some Dutch or Spanish master. I
heaped up this little Golden Age
for you to wake to, built a stage
on which we'd act our amorous parts
with strawberries, those redder hearts,

with melons, those fantastic breasts,
with grapes and mangoes and the rest;
you'd nibble cherries, bedhead-hung,
while I feasted with my tongue:
a couple from Fellini's kitsch
Satyricon, the bedroom rich
in sunlit colours and the scents
of fruits – and roses, deep, intense,

a crimson, velvet-petalled bunch . . .
Fruit would be our breakfast; lunch
would be more fruit, washed down with wine;
and we'd so twist and intertwine,
the bedroom would become a bower
and every passing sunlit hour
spent there, a bacchanal, baroque
and bronzed, a scene from *vieux Maroc*.

But in the restaurant that night
we quarrelled. Loss of appetite
drove our maddened voices on,
drink lent them venom. Gone
in a blazing instant, chair upturned,
you looked back once, and that look burned
its way into me – hot green knife,
lasering the source of life . . .

I moped my way back to the house
and all the time played cat-and-mouse
with my own thoughts. The stairs. The door.
And something touched the open sore
my mind had now become – the fruit!
The bowls of it, the senseless, brute
new fact that it would go to waste
with you not here, to eat, to taste!

I couldn't stand to see it plain,
to see each black grape ooze and stain
the room with accusation, each
pineapple, quumquat, plum and peach
grow overripe and rot. What use
those bleeding hearts, when all their juice
would pour itself out over no one's
mouth, what use those glowing suns

of mangoes, when there was no skin
to see their glow reflected in?
No more could I have thrown away
the feast I'd planned for us all day –
a pointless end, unplanned, unsought –
than I could cauterize my thought
of what a desert I had sown
in all that plenty . . . So, alone

in Barcelona for a week
I prowled the *barrio gotíc*
where you had lived two lonely years
and shed my solitary tears
in streets so full of you, I felt
your presence everywhere, and smelt
in every vaulted tapas bar
the strange amalgam that you are –

the sweet, the pungent and the salt.
Was I, I ask you now, at fault
to hear in the cathedral's hush
your whispered *Yes*, to see your flush
spreading as I stroked you? Was
I far beyond the pale because
I wanted you so much, I'd pause
before Picasso's minotaurs,

their bollocks taut, their massive cocks
like keys unlocking all the locks
in gaping, thick-thighed girls, and stare
as if I saw *you* lying there,
welcoming the hot intrusion?
If I saw, in my confusion,
Dalí's elongated globes
of female flesh, from arse to lobes,

as versions of the parts I missed,
distorted by the onanist's
grim fantasy – by mine as well,
since I was in a wanker's hell –
grotesquely stretched, like space, like time
itself, tormented by this crime
against love's natural law? No end
to long white nights without a friend . . .

And so I left for Paris, where
we'd clasped hands in the freezing air
and sat like breathing statues in
the Luxembourg, and watched the skin
grow darker on our *café-crèmes*
among the butches and the femmes
in Le Select, and gorged on love
and all the arty gossip of

the lunchtime ghosts in La Coupole;
but this time I could not be whole
or hungry, and each night I'd wake
and feel a sharp familiar ache
to have you there before I died –
to turn you over, slip inside
and fuck you, half-asleep; to feel
you feeding on me, while my meal

was what I savoured from behind,
the flesh, the pulp, the juice, the rind –
before I died one flophouse night,
oozing sour sweat, drink and fright,
staring into darkness, raw
and red-eyed, hating what I saw;
alone with shapes made by my shame
in pillows where I groaned your name.

By day the galleries I'd haunt –
shambling, spectral, shy and gaunt,
myself another kind of ghost –
showed me what I needed most:
Matisse's houris, Bonnard's Marthe
who glowed serenely in her bath
and, most of all, great Rodin's nudes –
the woman, real in all her moods

and manias, her ancient power
and beauty, offered for an hour,
a lifetime, to those lucky men
she chooses, then claimed back again
to please herself alone, her friends . . .
But none of these could make amends
for what I'd lost, or thrown away,
while Baudelaire and Hemingway,

Apollinaire and Gertrude Stein
all whispered of what had been mine.
Their voices told at every turn
the home truth that I had to learn:
I'd lost the thread, the plot, the way,
my *luxe*, my *calme*, my *volupté*;
I'd lost the object of my gaze,
the magnet of my nights, my days.

And Paris was, by day, by night
a monument to appetite,
to everything we crave, from sex
to food, from art to discothèques;
market-streets where stalls spilled fruit
in front of strollers; here, en route
from bar to adult cinema,
a woman splayed across a car;

there, to advertise a watch,
a pouting face, a pouting crotch;
shop windows stuffed with bras and pants
(the simulacra of romance),
with toys and leather, whips and creams
to smooth the passage of our dreams . . .
The films I watched dug deep in dirt.
I'd sit transfixed and tug and spurt

and sob to think I'd come so low.
How could I stay? How could I go
back home to what was waiting there,
the sweet corruption, foetid air,
the poisoned, seeping world I'd made?
I festered, shivering, afraid –
not of blackened fruit, not mould,
but the blacker tale they told:

of stupid anger, mindless haste,
of happiness that goes to waste.
I took the London train, to find
the fruit was mush, and mush my mind;
one thought wormed its way out: to mend
what I had broken, make an end
of breakfasts without you. Sit, eat
with me these first-fruits, bittersweet.

MURIEL STUART

In the Orchard

'I thought you loved me.' 'No, it was only fun.'
'When we stood there, closer than all?' 'Well, the harvest moon
Was shining and queer in your hair, and it turned my head.'
'That made you?' 'Yes.' 'Just the moon and the light it made
Under the tree?' 'Well, your mouth, too.' 'Yes, my mouth?'
'And the quiet there that sang like the drum in the booth.
You shouldn't have danced like that.' 'Like what?' 'So close,
With your head turned up, and the flower in your hair, a rose
That smelt all warm.' 'I loved you. I thought you knew
I wouldn't have danced like that with any but you.'
'I didn't know. I thought you knew it was fun.'
'I thought it was love you meant.' 'Well, it's done.' 'Yes, it's done.
I've seen boys stone a blackbird, and watched them drown
A kitten . . . it clawed at the reeds, and they pushed it down
Into the pool while it screamed. Is that fun, too?'
'Well, boys are like that . . . Your brothers . . .' 'Yes, I know.
But you, so lovely and strong! Not you! Not you!'
'They don't understand it's cruel. It's only a game.'
'And are girls fun, too?' 'No, still in a way it's the same.
It's queer and lovely to have a girl . . .' 'Go on.'
'It makes you mad for a bit to feel she's your own,
And you laugh and kiss her, and maybe you give her a ring,
But it's only in fun.' 'But I gave you everything.'
'Well, you shouldn't have done it. You know what a fellow thinks
When a girl does that.' 'Yes, he talks of her over his drinks
And calls her a—' 'Stop that now. I thought you knew.'
'But it wasn't with anyone else. It was only you.'
'How did I know? I thought you wanted it too.
I thought you were like the rest. Well, what's to be done?'

'To be done?' 'Is it all right?' 'Yes.' 'Sure?' 'Yes, but why?'
'I don't know. I thought you were going to cry.
You said you had something to tell me.' 'Yes, I know.
It wasn't anything really . . . I think I'll go.'
'Yes, it's late. There's thunder about, a drop of rain
Fell on my hand in the dark. I'll see you again
At the dance next week. You're sure that everything's right?'
'Yes.' 'Well, I'll be going.' 'Kiss me . . .' 'Good night.' . . .
'Good night.'

Chosen by Alan Jenkins

LINTON KWESI JOHNSON

Hurricane Blues

lang-time lovah
mi mine run pan yu all di while
an mi membah ow fus time
di two a wi come een – it did seem
like two shallow lickle snakin stream
mawchin mapless hapless a galang
tru di ruggid lanscape a di awt sang

an a soh wi did a gwaan
sohtil dat fateful day
awftah di pashan a di hurriance
furdah dan imaginaeshan ar dream
wi fine wiself lay-dung pan di same bedrack
flowin now togheddah as wan stream
ridin sublime tru love lavish terrain
lush an green an brite awftah di rain
shimmarin wid glittahrin eyes
glowin in di glare a di smilin sun

lang-time lovah
mi feel blue fi true wen mi tink bout yu
blue like di sky lingahrin pramis af rain
in di leakin lite in di hush af a evenin twilite
wen mi membah ow fus time
di two wi come een – it did seem
like a lang lang rivah dat is wide an deep

sometime wi woz silent like di langwidge a rackstone
sometime wi woodah sing wi rivah sang as wi a wine a galang
sometime wi jus cool an caam andah plenty shady tree
sometime sawfly lappin bamboo root as dem swing an sway
sometime cascadin carefree doun a steep gully bank
sometime turbulent in tempahment wi flood wi bank
but weddah ebb ar flow tru rain tru drout
wi nevah stra far fram love rigid route

ole-time sweet-awt
up til now mi still cyaan andahstan
ow wi get bag doun inna somuch silt an san
rackstone debri lag-jam
sohtil wi ad woz fi flow wi sepahret pawt
now traversin di tarrid terrain a love lanscape

runnin fram di polueshan af a cantrite awt
mi lang fi di marvelous miracle a hurricane
fi carry mi goh a meetin stream agen
lamentin mi saltid fate
sohmizin seh it too late

LORNA GOODISON

Poui

She don't put out for just anyone.
She waits for HIM
and in his high august heat
he takes her
and their celestial mating
is so intense
that for weeks her rose-gold dress
lies tangled round her feet
and she don't even notice.

Chosen by Linton Kwesi Johnson

Her

(for E.M.)

I had been told about her.
How she would always, always.
How she would never, never.
I'd watched and listened
but I still fell for her,
how she always, always.
How she never, never.

In the small brave night,
her lips, butterfly moments.
I tried to catch her and she laughed
a loud laugh that cracked me in two,
but then I had been told about her,
how she would always, always.
How she would never, never.

We two listened to the wind.
We two galloped a pace.
We two, up and away, away, away.
And now she's gone,
like she said she would go.
But then I had been told about her –
how she would always, always.

ROBERT BURNS

John Anderson My Jo

John Anderson my jo, John,
   When we were first acquent,
Your locks were like the raven,
   Your bonnie brow was brent;
But now your brow is beld, John,
   Your locks are like the snow;
But blessings on your frosty pow,
   John Anderson, my jo.

John Anderson my jo, John,
   We clamb the hill thegither;
And mony a canty day, John,
   We've had wi ane anither:
Now we maun totter down, John,
   And hand in hand we'll go,
And sleep thegither at the foot,
   John Anderson, my jo.

Chosen by Jackie Kay

BRENDAN KENNELLY

We Are Living

What is this room
But the moments we have lived in it?
When all due has been paid
To gods of wood and stone
And recognition has been made
Of those who'll breathe here when we are gone
Does it not take its worth from us
Who made it because we were here?

Your words are the only furniture I can remember
Your body the book that told me most.
If this room has a ghost
It will be your laughter in the frank dark
Revealing the world as a room
Loved only for those moments when
We touched the purely human.

I could give water now to thirsty plants,
Dig up the floorboards, the foundation,
Study the worm's confidence,
Challenge his omnipotence
Because my blind eyes have seen through walls
That make safe prisons of the days.

We are living
In ceiling, floor and windows,
We are given to where we have been.
This white door will always open
On what our hands have touched,
Our eyes have seen.

ROSEMARY TONKS

Story of a Hotel Room

Thinking we were safe – insanity.
We went to make love. All the same
Idiots to trust the little hotel bedroom.
Then in the gloom . . .
. . . And who does not know that pair of shutters
With the awkward hook on them
All screeching whispers? Very well then, in the gloom
We set about acquiring one another
Urgently. But on a temporary basis
Only as guests – just guests of one another's senses.

But idiots to feel so safe you hold back nothing
Because the bed of cold, electric linen
Happens to be illicit . . .
To make love as well as that is ruinous.
Londoner, Parisian, someone should have warned us
That without permanent intentions
You have absolutely no protection
– If the act is clean, authentic, sumptuous,
The concurring deep love of the heart
Follows the naked work, profoundly moved by it.

Chosen by Brendan Kennelly

TOM LEONARD

Touching Your Face

with that
silence

it creates
allowing

and
trusting

the allowed;
all that's

been said
and is saying

this time
breath

held
between us

each time
familiar

each time
new

A Fisher Idyll

Oh, saw ye bonnie Jean,
  In her braw blue duffle coat,
An' her little tartan shawl
  In a kink at her throat?
She's awa' doon to the pier
  To bring the line upbye;
For the yawls are comin' in,
  An' there's fish to fry.

Oh, I ken aboot a kist
  Fu' o' linen white as snaw!
An' ornaments an' orra things
  An dishes stowed awa'.
An' Willie, blythe an' young,
  Wi' nets an' gear forbye,
He looks, but ne'er lets on,
  When oor Jean gaes bye.

Oh, the lines are a' to bait,
  An' the mussels a' to sheel;
An' ower the limpit rocks
  She maun gang wi' her creel.
The nets are a' to mend,
  An' the hoose to redd an' clean;
But wi' love at her heart
  Naething daunts oor Jean.

A' the boats are gaun awa'
   Up the north to the drave;
An' Willie, young an' fain,
   Tries his luck wi' the lave.
But the little hoose is ta'en,
   And they say he's coft the ring;
Oh, Love! sae shy, sae sweet!
   Sing awa', lassie, sing!

Chosen by Tom Leonard

kist – chest *orra* – miscellaneous *sheel* – shell *redd* – tidy up
drave – shoal *lave* – the others, the rest *coft* – bought, purchased

In the edition of *Modern Scottish Poets* (thirteenth series, D. H. Edwards, Brechin 1890) from which this is taken, the entry for Jessie Kerr Lawson states that 'Mrs Lawson hails from St Monan's, Fife, and in her youth was a school teacher. After her marriage she went to Canada, her home and her family being still in Toronto. A writer of verse from the age of thirteen, her literary proclivities continued to crop up occasionally in spite of a busy life and the care of a large family.'

LIZ LOCHHEAD

Neckties

Paisleys squirm with spermatozoa.
All yang, no yin. Liberties are peacocks.
Old school types still hide behind their prison bars.
Red braces, jacquards, watermarked brocades
are the most fun a chap can have
in a sober suit.

You know about knots,
could tie, I bet, a bowtie properly
in the dark with your eyes shut, but
we've a diagram hung up
beside the mirror in our bedroom.
Left over right, et cetera . . .
The half or double Windsor,
even that extra fancy one it takes
an extra long tie to pull off successfully.
You know the times a simple schoolboy four-in-hand
will be what's wanted.

I didn't used to be married.
Once neckties were coiled occasional serpents
on the dressing-table by my bed
beside the car-keys and the teetering
temporary leaning towers of change.
They were dangerous nooses on the backs of chairs
or funny fishes in the debris on the floor.
I should have known better.

Picture me away from you
cruising the high streets
under the watchful eyes of shopboys
fingering their limp silks
wondering what would please you.
Watch out, someday I'll bring you back a naked lady,
a painted kipper, maybe a bootlace
dangling from a silver dollar
and matching collarpoints.
You could get away with anything
you're that good-looking.
Did you like that screenprinted slimjim from Convent Garden?

Once I got a beauty in a Cancer Shop
and a sort of forties effort in Oxfam for a song.
Not bad for one dull town.
The dead man's gravy stain wasn't the size of sixpence
and you can hide it behind your crocodile tie pin.

ROBERT BURNS

Mary Morison

O Mary, at thy window be,
　　It is the wish'd, the trysted hour;
Those smiles and glances let me see,
　　That make the miser's treasure poor:
How blythely wad I bide the stoure,
　　A weary slave frae sun to sun;
Could I the rich reward secure –
　　The lovely Mary Morison!

Yestreen, when to the trembling string,
　　The dance gaed thro' the lighted ha',
To thee my fancy took its wing,
　　I sat, but neither heard or saw:
Tho' this was fair, and that was braw,
　　And yon the toast of a' the town,
I sigh'd, and said amang them a',
　　'Ye are na Mary Morison.'

O Mary, canst thou wreck his peace,
　　Wha for thy sake wad gladly dee?
Or canst thou break that heart of his,
　　Whase only faut is loving thee?
If love for love thou wilt na gie,
　　At least be pity to me shown;
A though ungentle canna be
　　The thought o' Mary Morison.

Chosen by Liz Lochhead

Poem

If the night flights keep you awake
I will call London Airport and tell them
to land their dangerous junk elsewhere.

And if you fall asleep with the sleeve
of my jacket under your head,
sooner than wake you, I'll cut it off.

But if you say:
'Fix me a plug on this mixer',
I grumble and take my time.

A Letter

Lying in bed this morning, just a year
　　Since our first days, I was trying to assess –
Against my natural caution – by desire
　　And how the fact outdid it, my happiness:
And finding the awkwardness of keeping clear
　　　　Numberless flamingo thoughts and memories,
　　　　　　My dear and dearest husband, in this kind
　　　　　　Of rambling letter, I'll disburse my mind.

Technical problems have always given me trouble:
　　A child stiff at the fiddle, my ear had praise
And my intention only; so, as was natural,
　　Coming to verse, I hid my lack of ease
By writing only as I thought myself able,
　　　　Escaped the crash of the bold by salt originalities.
　　　　　　This is one reason for writing far from one's heart;
　　　　　　A better is, that one fears it may be hurt.

By an inadequate style one fears to cheapen
　　Glory, and that it may be blurred if seen
Through the eye's used centre, not the new margin.
　　It is the hardest thing with love to burn
And write it down, for what was the real passion
　　Left to its own words will seem trivial and thin.
　　　　We can in making love look face to face:
　　　　In poetry, crooked, and with no embrace.

Tolstoy's hero found in his newborn child
   Only another aching, vulnerable part;
And it is true our first joy hundredfold
   Increased our dangers, pricking in every street
In accidents and wars: yet this is healed
   Not by reason, but the endurance of delight
      Since our marriage, which, once thoroughly known,
      Is known for good, though in time it were gone.

You, hopeful baby with the erring toes,
   Grew, it seems to me, to a natural pleasure
In the elegant strict machine, from the abstruse
   Science of printing to the rich red and azure
It plays on hoardings, rusty industrial noise,
   All these could add to your inherited treasure:
      A poise which many wish for, writing the machine
      Poems of laboured praise, but few attain.

And loitered up your childhood to my arms.
   I would hold you there for ever, and know
Certainly now, that though the vacuum glooms,
   Quotidian dullness, in these beams don't die,
They're wrong who say that happiness never comes
   On earth, that has spread here its crystal sea.
      And since you, loiterer, did compose this wonder,
      Be with me still, and may God hold his thunder.

Chosen by Christopher Logue

The 'Singer'

In the evenings I used to study
At my mother's old sewing-machine,
Pressing my feet occasionally
Up and down on the treadle
As though I were going somewhere
I had never been.

Every year at exams, the pressure mounted –
The summer light bent across my pages
Like a squinting eye. The children's shouts
Echoed the weather of the street,
A car was thunder,
The ticking of a clock was heavy rain . . .

In the dark I drew the curtains
On young couples stopping in the entry,
Heading home. There were nights
I sent the disconnected wheel
Spinning madly round and round.
Till the empty bobbin rattled in its case.

The Spinning-Wheel Song

Mellow the moonlight to shine is beginning;
Close by the window young Eileen is spinning;
Bent o'er the fire, her blind grandmother, sitting,
Is croaning, and moaning, and drowsily knitting, –
'Eileen, a chora, I hear someone tapping.'
''T is the ivy, dear mother, against the glass flapping.'
'Eileen, I surely hear somebody sighing.'
''T is the sound, mother dear, of the summer wind dying.'

Merrily, cheerily, noisily whirring,
Swings the wheel, spins the wheel, while the foot's stirring;
Sprightly, and lightly, and airily ringing,
Thrills the sweet voice of the young maiden singing.

'What's that noise that I hear at the window, I wonder?'
''T is the little birds chirping the holly-bush under.'
'What makes you be shoving and moving your stool on,
And singing all wrong that old song of "The Coolun"?'
There's a form at the casement, the form of her true-love,
And he whispers, with face bent, 'I'm waiting for you, love;
Get up on the stool, through the lattice step lightly,
We'll rove in the grove while the moon's shining brightly.'

Merrily, cheerily, noisily whirring,
Swings the wheel, spins the reel, while the foot's stirring;
Sprightly, and lightly, and airily ringing,
Thrills the sweet voice of the young maiden singing.

The maid shakes her head, on her lip lays her fingers,
Steals up from her seat, – longs to go, and yet lingers;
A frightened glance turns to her drowsy grandmother,

Puts one foot on the stool, spins the wheel with the other.
Lazily, easily, swings now the wheel round;
Slowly and lowly is heard now the reel's sound;
Noiseless and light to the lattice above her
The maid steps, – then leaps to the arms of her lover.

Slower – and slower – and slower the wheel swings;
Lower – and lower – and lower the reel rings;
Ere the reel and the wheel stop their ringing and moving,
Through the grove the young lovers by moonlight are roving.

Chosen by Medbh McGuckian

Pillow Talk

These hot midsummer nights I whisper
assignations, trysts, heather beds
I'd like to lay you down in, remote beaches
we could escape to, watch
bonfire sparks mix with stars.
I want you to stay alive till we two
meet again, to hold the line, to ignore
the gossip traded about me in the marketplace,
I fall back on cliché, the small
change of an adulterous summer,
plots of half-hatched movies, theories
of forked lightning, how you make
the soles of my feet burn when I come.

What you don't hear is the other voice
when she speaks through me
beyond human pity or mercy. She wants you.
Put her eye on you the first time
she saw you. And I'm powerless,
a slave to her whim. She shall
have you. What can I do
when she speaks of white river stones,
elfin grots, her sacred birds?
I know she once tore a man apart,
limb from limb with her bare hands
in some rite in her bloody past.
My stomach turns at the hot
relentless stench of her history.

Nights you stare out
panic-stricken through the mask,
I think you may have heard her speak:
you realize that you ride a demon,
that the dark has no end to it.

Though I mean you no grief,
I cannot vouchsafe her intent. I fear
not all my healing arts can salve
the wound she has in store for you.

Miro's House for Lovers

My love, he writes, I have found us a house,
A farmhouse in Catalonia, such a house
As would shelter dreaming lovers.

There is a tree in the garden, rooted
In the void, shod in white enamel against goats.
It has leaves like the feathers of wet crows.

The ground floor was a stable once,
The top floor a granary. The windows are small,
Neat against wind and sun.

There is a lean-to with an old hooped wagon,
A cistern for drawing water, a columbarium.
And oh, the red, red earth of the garden!

Listen to me, the light is exactly right.
The letter of all beginnings could root in that light
Under a sky so blue the midday moon shines through.

Chosen by Paula Meehan

One Cigarette

No smoke without you, my fire.
After you left,
your cigarette glowed on in my ashtray
and sent up a long thread of such quiet grey
I smiled to wonder who would believe its signal
of so much love. One cigarette
in the non-smoker's tray.
As the last spire
trembles up, a sudden draught
blows it winding into my face.
Is it smell, is it taste?
You are here again, and I am drunk on your tobacco lips.
Out with the light.
Let the smoke lie back in the dark.
Till I hear the very ash
sigh down among the flowers of brass
I'll breathe, and long past midnight, your last kiss.

R. Alcona to J. Brenzaida*

Cold in the earth, and the deep snow piled above thee!
Far, far removed, cold in the dreary grave!
Have I forgot, my Only Love, to love thee,
Severed at last by Time's all-wearing wave?

Now, when alone, do my thoughts no longer hover
Over the mountains on Angora's shore;
Resting their wings where heath and fern-leaves cover
That noble heart for ever, ever more?

Cold in the earth, and fifteen wild Decembers
From those brown hills have melted into spring –
Faithful indeed is the spirit that remembers
After such years of change and suffering!

Sweet Love of youth, forgive if I forget thee
While the World's tide is bearing me along:
Sterner desires and darker hopes beset me,
Hopes which obscure but cannot do thee wrong.

No other Sun has lightened up my heaven;
No other Star has ever shone for me:
All my life's bliss from thy dear life was given –
All my life's bliss is in the grave with thee.

But when the days of golden dreams had perished
And even Despair was powerless to destroy,
Then did I learn how existence could be cherished,
Strengthened and fed without the aid of joy;

* Røsina Alcona to Julius Brenzaida.

Then did I check the tears of useless passion,
Weaned my young soul from yearning after thine;
Sternly denied its burning wish to hasten
Down to that tomb already more than mine!

And even yet, I dare not let it languish,
Dare not indulge in Memory's rapturous pain;
Once drinking deep of that divinest anguish,
How could I seek the empty world again?

Chosen by Edwin Morgan

Five Glimpses

The first glimpse, after hours standing,
put soles on my feet.

The second glimpse, after furious searching,
came to light under the edge of flesh,
it put soles on my feet.

The third glimpse was a horrible pain
located somewhere under the edge of flesh,
a glimmering sensation, a slight tremor of the hands,
it put soles on my feet.

The fourth glimpse, I began to recognise,
somewhere under the edge of flesh,
a glimmering sensation, a slight tremor of the hands
as if a golden thread was stitching my eyes
to the soles of my feet.

The last glimpse, I set out
through darkness, under the edge of flesh,
taking nothing but a slight tremor of the hands,
a thread threading the route;
a hundred years' walk, invoving every single bone
and the soles of my feet.

HUGH MacDIARMID

Back Bedroom

The dirty licht that through the winnock seeps
Into this unkempt room has glozed strange sichts;
Heaven like a Peepin' Tam 'twixt chimley-pots
Keeks i' the drab fore-nichts.

The folk that hed it last – the selfsame bed –
Were a great hulkin' cairter an' his bride.
She deed i' child-birth – on this verra spot
Whaur we'll lie side by side.

An' everything's deid-grey except oor een.
Wi' wee waugh jokes we strip an' intae bed . . .
An' suddenly oor een sing oot like stars
An' a' oor misery's shed.

What tho' the auld dour licht is undeceived?
What tho' a callous morn oure shairly comes?
For a wee while we ken but een like stars,
An' oor herts gaen' like drums.

Mony's the dreich back bedroom whaur the same
Sad little miracle tak's place ilk' nicht,
An' orra shapes o' sickly-hued mankind
Cheenge into forms o' licht.

Chosen by Alice Oswald

87

DON PATERSON

The Lover

(after Propertius)

Poor mortals, with your horoscopes and blood-tests –
what hope is there for you? Even if the plane
lands you safely, why should you not return
to your home in flames or ruins, your wife absconded,
the children blind and dying in their cots?
Even sitting quiet in a locked room
the perils are infinite and unforeseeable.
Only the lover walks upon the earth
careless of what the fates prepare for him:

so you step out at the lights, almost as if
you half-know that today you are the special one.
The woman in the windshield lifting away
her frozen cry, a white-mask on a stick,
reveals herself as grey-eyed Atropos;
the sun leaves like a rocket; the sky goes out;
the road floods and widens; on the distant kerb
the lost souls groan and mew like sad trombones;
the ambulance glides up with its black sail –

when somewhere in the other world, she fills
your name full of her breath again, and at once
you float to your feet: the dark rose on your shirt
folds itself away, and you slip back
into the crowd, who, being merely human,
must remember nothing of this incident.
Just one flea-ridden dog chained to the railing,
who might be Cerberus, or patient Argos,
looks on, knowing the great law you have flouted.

EDNA ST. VINCENT MILLAY

What Lips My Lips Have Kissed . . .

What lips my lips have kissed, and where, and why,
I have forgotten, and what arms have lain
Under my head till morning; but the rain
Is full of ghosts tonight, that tap and sigh
Upon the glass and listen for reply,
And in my heart there sits a quiet pain
For unremembered lads that not again
Will turn to me at midnight with a cry.
Thus in the winter stands the lonely tree,
Nor knows what birds have vanished one by one,
Yet knows its boughs more silent than before:
I cannot say what loves have come and gone,
I only know that summer sang in me
A little while, that in me sings no more.

Chosen by Don Paterson

DERYN REES-JONES

The Fish

'Rainbow, rainbow, rainbow!'
(E.B.)

I go to sleep with the taste of you, and this is not the first time

for you are too much with me. And these are your hands,
in the darkness. This is the rough shape of
your face, only. Your hair, your ear, your thigh.
          And then, out of nowhere, your tongue like a hot little fish
a blue fish, glinted electrics,
a fish accustomed to basking, I suppose,
in the clear hot waters of some tropical isle.
Not an ordinary fish, not a fish I could haul from the waters, or
          not easily.
Not a fish accustomed to travelling in solitude,
but one used to a rainbow accompaniment,
one used to the sea's depths, and her sulky harbourings.
One used to the rockpools and the undertow, the colour of the
          sands.
And, how suddenly you swam into me!
          And was it your mouth, or the memory of your mouth?
Or was it a fish? Whatever it was, it was there.
There in the bloodstream, bruising artery, vein,
as it swam,
heading, no doubt, for the heart.
Then you stopped it,
          for you knew it would have killed me,
and it basked in the blue pools of my elbow, where you
stroked it for a while;

91

then you asked it to dart, from my hips up my spine,
you asked it to wander to the tilt of my breastbone
where tickled, like a salmon, it leapt
      it leapt;
you asked it to journey from my shoulder to my neck, to that soft
         place
behind my ears
where you solemnly forbade it, asked it instead to
rest for a while, and then turn back,
sayings *Fish, fish, my brilliant fish*
      and something I can't
remember now

on the furthermost tip of my tongue, like a dream.

SEAMUS HEANEY

The Skunk

Up, black, striped and damasked like the chasuble
At a funeral mass, the skunk's tail
Paraded the skunk. Night after night
I expected her like a visitor.

The refrigerator whinnied into silence.
My desk light softened beyond the veranda.
Small oranges loomed in the orange tree.
I began to be tense as a voyeur.

After eleven years I was composing
Love-letters again, broaching the word 'wife'
Like a stored cask, as if its slender vowel
Had mutated into the night earth and air

Of California. The beautiful, useless
Tang of eucalyptus spelt your absence.
The aftermath of a mouthful of wine
Was like inhaling you off a cold pillow.

And there she was, the intent and glamorous,
Ordinary, mysterious skunk,
Mythologized, demythologized,
Snuffing the boards five feet beyond me.

It all came back to me last night, stirred
By the sootfall of your things at bedtime,
Your head-down, tail-up hunt in a bottom drawer
For the black plunge-line nightdress.

Chosen by Deryn Rees-Jones

CAROL RUMENS

In the Season of Green Gowns

Summer will take from you everything I desire:
It will pluck at your sleeve, quietly undo
A handful of buttons, seeking no disclosure
That wasn't first fully consented to,
As you walked and turned in your mirror's candid gaze
And wouldn't be rushed. Summer, shyly approving,
Will lead you from chaste decision to easy living.

Summer will tell me what I could never enquire:
The pale length of your arm, sleeved in its years,
The freckled blush at the wrist. Summer confirms
The less-than-perfect as our most tender haunting.
It pours my desire into the depth of the mould
Like a conception. But, like a man or a child,
I simply can't tell if you are filled or wanting.

Ca' the Yowes to the Knowes

Chorus
Ca' the yowes to the knowes,
    Ca' them whare the heather grows,
Ca' them whare the burnie rowes,
        My bonie Dearie.

Hark, the mavis' evening sang
Sounding Clouden's woods amang;
Then a faulding let us gang,
        My bonie Dearie.
    Ca' the &c.

We'll gae down by Clouden side,
Through the hazels spreading wide
O'er the waves, that sweetly glide
        To the moon sae clearly.
    Ca' the &c.

Yonder Clouden's silent towers,
Where at moonshine midnight hours
O'er the dewy bending flowers
        Fairies dance sae cheary.
    Ca' the &c.

Ghaist nor bogle shalt thou fear;
Thou'rt to Love and Heaven sae dear,
Nocht of Ill may come thee near,
        My bonie Dearie.
    Ca' the &c.

Fair and lovely as thou art,
Thou hast stown my very heart;
I can die – but canna part,
   My bonie Dearie.
 Ca' the &c.

Chosen by Carol Rumens

JO SHAPCOTT

Muse

When I kiss you in all the folding places
of your body, you make that noise like a dog
dreaming, dreaming of the long runs he makes
in answer to some jolt to his hormones,
running across landfills, running, running
by tips and shorelines from the scent of too much
but still going with head up and snout
in the air because he loves it all
and has to get away. I have to kiss deeper
and more slowly – your neck, your inner arm,
the neat creases under your toes, the shadow
behind your knee, the white angles of your groin –
until you fall quiet because only then
can I get the damned words to come into my mouth.

SIR PHILIP SIDNEY

Astrophel and Stella: I

Loving in truth, and fain in verse my love to show,
that she, dear she, might take some pleasure of my pain, –
Pleasure might cause her read, reading might make her know,
Knowledge might pity win, and pity grace obtain, –
I sought fit words to paint the blackest face of woe;
Studying inventions fine her wits to entertain,
Oft turning others' leaves, to see if thence would flow
Some fresh and fruitful showers upon my sunburn'd brain.
But words came halting forth, wanting invention's stay;
Invention, Nature's child, fled step-dame Study's blows;
And others' feet still seem'd but strangers in my way.
Thus great with child to speak and helpless in my throes,
Biting my truant pen, beating myself for spite,
'Fool,' said my Muse to me, 'look in thy heart, and write.'

Chosen by Jo Shapcott

MATTHEW SWEENEY

The Bridal Suite

On the third night in the bridal suite
without the bride, he panicked.
He couldn't handle another dream like that,
not wet, like he'd expected,
but not dry either – men digging holes
that they'd fill with water, donkeys
crossing valleys that suddenly flooded.
The alarm-call had a job to wake him,
to send him out from the huge bed,
past the corner kissing-sofa, up two steps
to the shower he hardly needed,
where he'd scrub himself clean as the baby
he'd hoped to start that night,
under the canopy like a wimple,
in that room of pinks and greens.
Naked and dripping, he'd rung Reception
to see if she'd rung, then he'd stood
looking out at the new marina,
as if he'd glimpse her on a yacht.
On the third night he could take no more –
he dressed, to the smell of her perfume,
and leaving her clothes there,
the wedding dress in a pile in the wardrobe,
he walked past the deaf night porter,
out to his car. He had no idea
where he was headed, only that she,

if she ever came back, could sample
the bridal suite on her own,
could toss in that canopied bed
and tell him about her dreams.

CHASE TWICHELL

The Condom Tree

Pleasure must slip
right through memory's barbed wire,
because sex makes lost things reappear.
This afternoon when I shut my eyes
beneath his body's heavy braille,
I fell through the rosy darkness
all the way back to my tenth year,
the year of the secret
place by the river,
where the old dam spilled
long ropes of water and the froth
chafed the small stones smooth.
I looked up and there it was,
a young maple
still raw in early spring,
and drooping pale
from every reachable branch
dozens of latex blooms.
I knew what they were,
that the older kids
had hung them there,
but the tree – was it beautiful,
caught in that dirty floral light,
or was it an ugly thing?
Beautiful first, and ugly afterward,
when I saw up close
the shriveled human skins?
That must be right,
though in the remembering

its value has been changed again,
and now that flowering
dapples the two of us
with its tendered shadows,
dapples the rumpled bed as it slips
out of the damp present
into our separate pasts.

Chosen by Matthew Sweeney

HUGO WILLIAMS

The Lisboa

Pass me the alarm clock, Carolyn.
What time do you have to go to work?
I'll set it for half past seven,
then we'll have time for breakfast.
I'll get the milk.

Listen, why don't you ring up in the morning
and say you're going to be late?
Then we can do what we like.
We could go to the Lisboa and have custard tarts.
We could go to the Gate.

Lift up your arms.
Let me take this off.

EVA SALZMAN

Sexual Love

The motorboat's charge
trickles to shore, diminishing.
The bay tends back towards peace.

And that's why I like it;
though clamming by foot takes time,
a certain readjustment of the will.

At first, the mud's unwearable
for its soft give, the deepening
silent rip of ancient silk:

the way it clings around the ankles,
will never tear, or tears
repeatedly, the old healing.

Chosen by Hugo Williams

Acknowledgements

The editor and publishers wish to thank the following for permission to use copyright material:

Fleur Adcock – 'An Illustration to Dante' from *Poems 1960–2000* by Fleur Adcock (2000), by permission of Bloodaxe Books.

Moniza Alvi – 'A Bowl of Warm Air' from *Carrying My Wife* by Moniza Alvi (2000), by permission of Bloodaxe Books.

Anon – 'My Heart Burns for Him', translated by S. Hirvale and V. Elwin, Allen & Unwin (1935), by permission of Routledge.

Simon Armitage – 'To His Lost Lover' from *Book of Matches* by Simon Armitage, by permission of Faber and Faber Ltd.

Elizabeth Bishop – 'The Shampoo' from *The Complete Poems 1927–1979* by Elizabeth Bishop. Copyright © 1979, 1983 by Alice Helen Methfessel, by permission of Farrar, Straus and Giroux, LLC.

Colette Bryce – 'Song for a Stone', by permission of the author.

C. P. Cavafy – 'Come Back' from *Collected Poems*, translated by Edmund Keeley and Philip Sherrard, Chatto & Windus, by permission of Random House Group Ltd.

Kate Clanchy – 'Patagonia' from *Slattern* by Kate Clanchy, by permission of the author.

Gillian Clarke – 'Gravity', by permission of the author.

Billy Collins – 'Japan' from *Picnic, Lightning* by Billy Collins. Copyright © 1998, by permission of the University of Pittsburgh Press.

Robert Crawford – 'Conjugation', by permission of the author.

Kathleen Jamie – 'Perfect Day' from *The Queen of Sheba* by Kathleen Jamie (1994), by permission of Bloodaxe Books.

Alan Jenkins – 'The Breakfast', by permission of the author.

Linton Kwesi Johnson – 'Hurricane Blues', by permission of LKJ Music (Publishers) Ltd.

Jackie Kay – 'Her', by permission of the author.

Brendan Kennelly – 'We Are Living' from *A Time for Voices: Selected Poems 1960–1990* by Brendan Kennelly (1990), by permission of Bloodaxe Books.

Dorianne Laux – 'Kissing' from *What We Carry* by Dorianne Laux. Copyright © 1994 by Dorianne Laux, by permission of BOA Editions, Ltd.

Tom Leonard – 'Touching Your Face', by permission of the author.

Liz Lochhead – 'Neckties' from *Bagpipe Muzak* by Liz Lochhead (1991). Copyright © 1991 by Liz Lochhead, by permission of Penguin Books Ltd.

Christopher Logue – 'Poem (If the night flights . . .)' from *Selected Poems* by Christopher Logue (1996), by permission of Faber and Faber Ltd.

Michael Longley – 'The Linen Industry', by permission of Peters Fraser & Dunlop Group Ltd on behalf of the author.

Hugh MacDiarmid – 'Back Bedroom' from *Complete Poems Vol. 2* by Hugh MacDiarmid (1994), by permission of Carcanet Press.

Medbh McGuckian – 'The "Singer"' from *The Flower Master and Other Poems* by Medbh McGuckian, by permission of The Gallery Press.

Paula Meehan – 'Pillow Talk' from *Pillow Talk* by Paula Meehan (1994), by permission of The Gallery Press.

Edwin Morgan – 'One Cigarette' from *Collected Poems* by Edwin Morgan (1990), by permission of Carcanet Press.

Pablo Neruda – 'We Have Lost Even' from *20 Love Poems and a Song of Despair* by Pablo Neruda, translated by W. S. Merwin, Jonathan Cape (1969), by permission of Random House Group Ltd.

Nuala Ní Dhomhnaill – 'Labysheedy (The Silken Bed)', by permission of the author, c/o The Gallery Press.

Sean O'Brien – 'Indian Summer' from *Downriver*, Macmillan (2001), by permission of the author.

Alice Oswald – 'Five Glimpses', by permission of the author.

Ruth Padel – 'Tell Me about It' from *Fusewire*, Chatto & Windus (1996), by permission of Random House Group Ltd.

Don Paterson – 'The Lover' from *God's Gift to Women* by Don Paterson, by permission of Faber and Faber Ltd.

Zsuzsa Rakovszky – 'They Were Burning Dead Leaves' from *New Life* by Zsuzsa Rakovszky, translated by George Szirtes (1994). Copyright © Zsuzsa Rakovszky 1981, 1987, 1991, by permission of Oxford University Press.

Deryn Rees-Jones – 'The Fish' from *Signs Round a Dead Body* by Deryn Rees-Jones (1998), by permission of Seren Books.

Anne Ridler – 'A Letter' from *Collected Poems* (1994), by permission of Carcanet Press.

Carol Rumens – 'In the Season of Green Gowns' from *Thinking of Skins: New and Selected Poems* by Carol Rumens (1993), by permission of Bloodaxe Books.

Eva Salzman – 'Sexual Love' from *Bargain with the Watchman*, Oxford University Press (1997), by permission of the author.

Delmore Schwartz – 'What Is to Be Given' from *Selected Poems* by Delmore Schwartz, New Directions Publishing Corporation, by permission of Laurence Pollinger Ltd on behalf of the author.

Jo Shapcott – 'Muse' from *Her Book* by Jo Shapcott, by permission of Faber and Faber Ltd.

Stevie Smith – 'Infelice', by permission of James and James (Publishers) Ltd, Executors of the Estate of James MacGibbon.

Edna St Vincent Millay – 'What Lips My Lips Have Kissed'. Copyright © The Estate of the Late Edna St Vincent Millay, by permission of A. M. Heath & Co Ltd on behalf of the Estate of the author.

Muriel Stuart – 'In the Orchard', by permission of E. A. Stapleforth.

Matthew Sweeney – 'The Bridal Suite' from *The Bridal Suite*, Jonathan Cape, by permission of Random House Group Ltd.

Chase Twichell – 'The Condom Tree' from *Perdido* by Chase Twichell, by permission of Faber and Faber Ltd.

Hugo Williams – 'The Lisboa' from *Billy's Rain* by Hugo Williams, by permission of Faber and Faber Ltd.

Judith Wright – 'The Twins' from *A Human Pattern: Selected Poems* by Judith Wright (1996), by permission of ETT Imprint, Sydney.

W. B. Yeats – 'Solomon and the Witch', by permission of A. P. Watt Ltd on behalf of Michael B. Yeats.

Every effort has been made to trace the copyright holders but if any have been inadvertently overlooked the publishers will be pleased to make the necessary arrangement at the first opportunity.

Index of Poets

Index of Titles

Index of First Lines